FLUTE

BIG BOOK

of

Disney

SONGS

T0084192

Available for
FLUTE, CLARINET, ALTO SAX, TENOR SAX, TRUMPET,
HORN, TROMBONE, VIOLIN, VIOLA, CELLO

ISBN 978-1-4584-1131-0

Walt Disney Music Company
Wonderland Music Company, Inc.

DISTRIBUTED BY

HAL•LEONARD®
CORPORATION

7777 W. BLUEMOUND RD. P.O. BOX 13819 MILWAUKEE, WI 53213

In Australia Contact:
Hal Leonard Australia Pty. Ltd.
4 Lentara Court
Cheltenham, Victoria, 3192 Australia
Email: ausadmin@halleonard.com.au

Visit Hal Leonard Online at
www.halleonard.com

CONTENTS

4 Alice in Wonderland

4 The Ballad of Davy Crockett

6 The Bare Necessities

5 Be Our Guest

7 Beauty and the Beast

8 Bella Notte (This Is the Night)

12 Best of Friends

8 Bibbidi-Bobbidi-Boo

10 Breaking Free

13 Can You Feel the Love Tonight

14 Candle on the Water

15 Chim Chim Cher-ee

18 Circle of Life

16 Colors of the Wind

9 Cruella De Vil

17 A Dream Is a Wish Your Heart Makes

20 Friend Like Me

19 Go the Distance

22 God Help the Outcasts

24 Hakuna Matata

25 He's a Tramp

23 How D'ye Do and Shake Hands

26 I Just Can't Wait to Be King

27 I'm Late

28 If I Never Knew You

30 It's a Small World

36 Kiss the Girl

30 Lavender Blue (Dilly Dilly)

31 Let's Get Together

32 Let's Go Fly a Kite

34 Little April Shower

34 The Lord Is Good to Me

35 Mickey Mouse March

32 My Funny Friend and Me

37 Never Smile at a Crocodile

40 Once upon a Dream

38 Part of Your World

42 A Pirate's Life

40 Reflection

44 Saludos Amigos

42 Scales and Arpeggios

43 The Second Star to the Right

46 The Siamese Cat Song

45 So This Is Love

48 Someday

49 Someone's Waiting for You

46 Sooner or Later

50 A Spoonful of Sugar

56 Supercalifragilisticexpialidocious

52 Sweet Surrender

51 These Are the Best Times

53 Toyland March

54 Trashin' the Camp

57 The Unbirthday Song

58 Under the Sea

60 We're All in This Together

55 Westward Ho, The Wagons!

68 A Whale of a Tale

62 When She Loved Me

64 Where the Dream Takes You

66 A Whole New World

63 Winnie the Pooh

68 The Wonderful Thing About Tiggers

70 Wringle Wrangle (A Pretty Woman's Love)

71 Written in the Stars

69 Yo Ho (A Pirate's Life for Me)

72 You Are the Music in Me

76 You Can Fly! You Can Fly! You Can Fly!

74 You'll Be in My Heart (Pop Version)

77 You've Got a Friend in Me

78 Zero to Hero

80 Zip-A-Dee-Doo-Dah

ALICE IN WONDERLAND
from Walt Disney's ALICE IN WONDERLAND

Flute

Words by BOB HILLIARD
Music by SAMMY FAIN

THE BALLAD OF DAVY CROCKETT
from Walt Disney's DAVY CROCKETT

Words by TOM BLACKBURN
Music by GEORGE BRUNS

BE OUR GUEST
from Walt Disney's BEAUTY AND THE BEAST

Lyrics by HOWARD ASHMAN
Music by ALAN MENKEN

Moderately

THE BARE NECESSITIES

from Walt Disney's THE JUNGLE BOOK

FLUTE

Words and Music by
TERRY GILKYSON

BEAUTY AND THE BEAST

from Walt Disney's BEAUTY AND THE BEAST

Flute

Lyrics by HOWARD ASHMAN
Music by ALAN MENKEN

FLUTE

BELLA NOTTE
(This Is the Night)
from Walt Disney's LADY AND THE TRAMP

Words and Music by PEGGY LEE
and SONNY BURKE

BIBBIDI-BOBBIDI-BOO
(The Magic Song)
from Walt Disney's CINDERELLA

Words by JERRY LIVINGSTON
Music by MACK DAVID and AL HOFFMAN

CRUELLA DE VIL

from Walt Disney's 101 DALMATIANS

Words and Music by
MEL LEVEN

BREAKING FREE

from the Disney Channel Original Movie HIGH SCHOOL MUSICAL

Flute

Words and Music by
JAMIE HOUSTON

Moderately

BEST OF FRIENDS
from Walt Disney's THE FOX AND THE HOUND

Flute

Words by STAN FIDEL
Music by RICHARD JOHNSTON

Moderately

CAN YOU FEEL THE LOVE TONIGHT

from Walt Disney Pictures' THE LION KING

Flute

Music by ELTON JOHN
Lyrics by TIM RICE

Pop Ballad

CANDLE ON THE WATER

from Walt Disney's PETE'S DRAGON

Flute

Words and Music by AL KASHA
and JOEL HIRSCHHORN

Spiritually

CHIM CHIM CHER-EE

from Walt Disney's MARY POPPINS

Flute

Words and Music by RICHARD M. SHERMAN
and ROBERT B. SHERMAN

COLORS OF THE WIND

from Walt Disney's POCAHONTAS

Flute

Music by ALAN MENKEN
Lyrics by STEPHEN SCHWARTZ

A DREAM IS A WISH YOUR HEART MAKES

from Walt Disney's CINDERELLA

Words and Music by MACK DAVID,
AL HOFFMAN and JERRY LIVINGSTON

CIRCLE OF LIFE
from Walt Disney Pictures' THE LION KING

FLUTE

Music by ELTON JOHN
Lyrics by TIM RICE

Moderately (with an African beat)

GO THE DISTANCE

from Walt Disney Pictures' HERCULES

FLUTE

Music by ALAN MENKEN
Lyrics by DAVID ZIPPEL

FRIEND LIKE ME

from Walt Disney's ALADDIN

FLUTE

Lyrics by HOWARD ASHMAN
Music by ALAN MENKEN

GOD HELP THE OUTCASTS

from Walt Disney's THE HUNCHBACK OF NOTRE DAME

Flute

Music by ALAN MENKEN
Lyrics by STEPHEN SCHWARTZ

HOW D'YE DO AND SHAKE HANDS

from Walt Disney's ALICE IN WONDERLAND

Words by CY COBEN
Music by OLIVER WALLACE

HAKUNA MATATA

from Walt Disney Pictures' THE LION KING

FLUTE

Music by ELTON JOHN
Lyrics by TIM RICE

HE'S A TRAMP
from Walt Disney's LADY AND THE TRAMP

Words and Music by PEGGY LEE
and SONNY BURKE

Moderately

I JUST CAN'T WAIT TO BE KING

from Walt Disney Pictures' THE LION KING

Flute

Music by ELTON JOHN
Lyrics by TIM RICE

I'M LATE

from Walt Disney's ALICE IN WONDERLAND

Words by BOB HILLIARD
Music by SAMMY FAIN

Moderately fast

IF I NEVER KNEW YOU
(Love Theme from POCAHONTAS)
from Walt Disney's POCAHONTAS

Flute

Music by ALAN MENKEN
Lyrics by STEPHEN SCHWARTZ

Moderately slow

IT'S A SMALL WORLD

from Disneyland Resort® and Magic Kingdom® Park

FLUTE

Words and Music by RICHARD M. SHERMAN
and ROBERT B. SHERMAN

LAVENDER BLUE

(Dilly Dilly)

from Walt Disney's SO DEAR TO MY HEART

Words by LARRY MOREY
Music by ELIOT DANIEL

LET'S GET TOGETHER

from Walt Disney Pictures' THE PARENT TRAP

Words and Music by RICHARD M. SHERMAN
and ROBERT B. SHERMAN

Moderate Rock

LET'S GO FLY A KITE

from Walt Disney's MARY POPPINS

Flute

Words and Music by RICHARD M. SHERMAN
and ROBERT B. SHERMAN

MY FUNNY FRIEND AND ME

from Walt Disney Pictures' THE EMPEROR'S NEW GROOVE

Lyrics by STING
Music by STING and DAVID HARTLEY

LITTLE APRIL SHOWER
from Walt Disney's BAMBI

FLUTE

Words by LARRY MOREY
Music by FRANK CHURCHILL

THE LORD IS GOOD TO ME
from Walt Disney's MELODY TIME
from Walt Disney's JOHNNY APPLESEED

Words and Music by KIM GANNON
and WALTER KENT

MICKEY MOUSE MARCH

from Walt Disney's THE MICKEY MOUSE CLUB

Words and Music by
JIMMIE DODD

KISS THE GIRL

from Walt Disney's THE LITTLE MERMAID

FLUTE

Music by ALAN MENKEN
Lyrics by HOWARD ASHMAN

NEVER SMILE AT A CROCODILE

from Walt Disney's PETER PAN

Words by JACK LAWRENCE
Music by FRANK CHURCHILL

PART OF YOUR WORLD
from Walt Disney's THE LITTLE MERMAID

FLUTE

Music by ALAN MENKEN
Lyrics by HOWARD ASHMAN

ONCE UPON A DREAM
from Walt Disney's SLEEPING BEAUTY

FLUTE

Words and Music by SAMMY FAIN
and JACK LAWRENCE
Adapted from a Theme by Tchaikovsky

REFLECTION
from Walt Disney Pictures' MULAN

Music by MATTHEW WILDER
Lyrics by DAVID ZIPPEL

A PIRATE'S LIFE
from Walt Disney's PETER PAN

FLUTE

Words by ED PENNER
Music by OLIVER WALLACE

SCALES AND ARPEGGIOS
from Walt Disney's THE ARISTOCATS

Words and Music by RICHARD M. SHERMAN
and ROBERT B. SHERMAN

THE SECOND STAR TO THE RIGHT

from Walt Disney's PETER PAN

Words by SAMMY CAHN
Music by SAMMY FAIN

SALUDOS AMIGOS

from Walt Disney's SALUDOS AMIGOS
from Walt Disney's THE THREE CABALLEROS

Flute

Words by NED WASHINGTON
Music by CHARLES WOLCOTT

SO THIS IS LOVE
(The Cinderella Waltz)
from Walt Disney's CINDERELLA

FLUTE

Words and Music by MACK DAVID,
AL HOFFMAN and JERRY LIVINGSTON

THE SIAMESE CAT SONG

from Walt Disney's LADY AND THE TRAMP

FLUTE

Words and Music by PEGGY LEE
and SONNY BURKE

SOONER OR LATER

from Walt Disney's SONG OF THE SOUTH

Words and Music by RAY GILBERT
and CHARLES WOLCOTT

(knock, knock)

(knock, knock)

SOMEDAY

from Walt Disney's THE HUNCHBACK OF NOTRE DAME

Flute

Music by ALAN MENKEN
Lyrics by STEPHEN SCHWARTZ

SOMEONE'S WAITING FOR YOU

from Walt Disney's THE RESCUERS

Flute

Words by CAROL CONNORS and AYN ROBBINS
Music by SAMMY FAIN

A SPOONFUL OF SUGAR

from Walt Disney's MARY POPPINS

FLUTE

Words and Music by RICHARD M. SHERMAN
and ROBERT B. SHERMAN

THESE ARE THE BEST TIMES

from Walt Disney Productions' SUPERDAD

FLUTE

Words and Music by
SHANE TATUM

SWEET SURRENDER

from Walt Disney's THE BEARS AND I

FLUTE

Words and Music by
JOHN DENVER

TOYLAND MARCH

from Walt Disney's BABES IN TOYLAND

Adapted from V. HERBERT Melody
Words by MEL LEVEN
Music by GEORGE BRUNS

March tempo

TRASHIN' THE CAMP

from Walt Disney Pictures' TARZAN™

FLUTE

Words and Music by
PHIL COLLINS

Moderate Swing

Wooh!

Gradually faster

Wooh!

Wooh! *Wooh!*

Wooh! *Wooh!*

Wooh!

WESTWARD HO, THE WAGONS!

from Walt Disney's WESTWARD HO, THE WAGONS!

Words by TOM BLACKBURN
Music by GEORGE BRUNS

Lively

SUPERCALIFRAGILISTICEXPIALIDOCIOUS

from Walt Disney's MARY POPPINS

FLUTE

Words and Music by RICHARD M. SHERMAN
and ROBERT B. SHERMAN

THE UNBIRTHDAY SONG

from Walt Disney's ALICE IN WONDERLAND

Flute

Words and Music by MACK DAVID,
AL HOFFMAN and JERRY LIVINGSTON

UNDER THE SEA
from Walt Disney's THE LITTLE MERMAID

FLUTE

Music by ALAN MENKEN
Lyrics by HOWARD ASHMAN

WE'RE ALL IN THIS TOGETHER

from the Disney Channel Original Movie HIGH SCHOOL MUSICAL

Flute

Words and Music by MATTHEW GERRARD
and ROBBIE NEVIL

WHEN SHE LOVED ME

from Walt Disney Pictures' TOY STORY 2 - A Pixar Film

Flute

Music and Lyrics by
RANDY NEWMAN

Tenderly, very freely

WINNIE THE POOH

from Walt Disney's THE MANY ADVENTURES OF WINNIE THE POOH

Words and Music by RICHARD M. SHERMAN
and ROBERT B. SHERMAN

Tenderly

WHERE THE DREAM TAKES YOU

from Walt Disney Pictures' ATLANTIS: THE LOST EMPIRE

FLUTE

Lyrics by DIANE WARREN
Music by DIANE WARREN
and JAMES NEWTON HOWARD

A WHOLE NEW WORLD

from Walt Disney's ALADDIN

FLUTE

Music by ALAN MENKEN
Lyrics by TIM RICE

A WHALE OF A TALE

from Walt Disney's 20,000 LEAGUES UNDER THE SEA

FLUTE

Words and Music by NORMAN GIMBEL
and AL HOFFMAN

With a bounce

THE WONDERFUL THING ABOUT TIGGERS

from Walt Disney's THE MANY ADVENTURES OF WINNIE THE POOH

Words and Music by RICHARD M. SHERMAN
and ROBERT B. SHERMAN

Very brightly

YO HO
(A Pirate's Life for Me)
from PIRATES OF THE CARIBBEAN at Disneyland Park and Magic Kingdom Park

Words by XAVIER ATENCIO
Music by GEORGE BRUNS

WRINGLE WRANGLE

(A Pretty Woman's Love)

from Walt Disney's WESTWARD HO, THE WAGONS!

FLUTE

Words and Music by
STAN JONES

Lively

(whistle) Hey! (slap leg)

(whistle) Hey! (slap leg)

(whistle) Hey! (slap leg)

1.

2.

(whistle) Hey! (slap leg)

WRITTEN IN THE STARS

from Elton John and Tim Rice's AIDA

FLUTE

Music by ELTON JOHN
Lyrics by TIM RICE

YOU ARE THE MUSIC IN ME

from the Disney Channel Original Movie HIGH SCHOOL MUSICAL 2

FLUTE

Words and Music by
JAMIE HOUSTON

YOU'LL BE IN MY HEART

(Pop Version)

from Walt Disney Pictures' TARZAN™

FLUTE

Words and Music by
PHIL COLLINS

YOU CAN FLY! YOU CAN FLY! YOU CAN FLY!

from Walt Disney's PETER PAN

FLUTE

Words by SAMMY CAHN
Music by SAMMY FAIN

YOU'VE GOT A FRIEND IN ME

from Walt Disney's TOY STORY

Flute

Music and Lyrics by
RANDY NEWMAN

ZERO TO HERO
from Walt Disney Pictures' HERCULES

FLUTE

Music by ALAN MENKEN
Lyrics by DAVID ZIPPEL

ZIP-A-DEE-DOO-DAH

from Walt Disney's SONG OF THE SOUTH

Flute

Words by RAY GILBERT
Music by ALLIE WRUBEL